The Formula for Branding

Terms and Conditions

Table Of Contents

Foreword

Branding is very similar to advertising but at a deeper level. Branding is about encouraging a potential customer to seriously consider a product by the fact that the said product is uniquely different and better than its competitors.

In the current "market place" where there are so many products to choose from, it can get quite competitive, thus attracting the customer to stay loyal or consider and alternative product is very important.

The Branding Formula

Learn How To Brand Yourself As An Expert In Any Niche And Profit
Big Time

Chapter 1:

Just What Is Branding

Synopsis

Getting the message across to the customer clearly and quickly is the first point to ensure, if the said product is to succeed in the competitive market arena. Good branding styles will attract the customer base needed to ensure high sales targets achieved.

Some Basic Info

Good branding styles also helps to confirm the credibility of the product advertised. If the product has a few competitors, as most products do, there is a need to ensure the customer is very aware of the benefits in making a particular choice. This is where the branding element comes in.

Being able to connect with a potential customer on a more personal level of emotional level is definitely an advantage. Therefore good branding styles needs to focus on making the sales pitch based on these sentiments.

As most products are displayed together, the product that has the most branding promotions will probably make a better impact on the potential customer. When the branding message is firmly imprinted in the mind of the potential customer, this element will help to ensure the customer stays motivated to pick that particular product.

Ensuring the loyalty of a customer stays consistent, is another reason to ensure branding is part of the promotional style of a product. With constant changes and new products being available, keeping the customer focus and loyal is an uphill battle. The branding style must be competitive and effective.

Chapter 2:

Research Your Topic Thoroughly

Synopsis

Basically this entails being as knowledgeable as possible, on a particular product or service. This element is very important especially in the product branding arena.

If a product or service is not well researched then the advertising campaign which includes effective branding styles will end up being inadequate and ineffective. Worse still if the information used in the branding is incorrect or misleading, the negative repercussion can be phenomenally damaging.

Know All You Can

It would be wise to use the following steps as a guide to thoroughly researching a product to ensure accurate and effective branding styles.

Market observation and the eventual preparation of a complete portfolio on the product or service must be compiled. The observations conducted to understand the needs and reasons the potential customer chooses and uses a particular product is important to ensure this information is used to the maximum advantage in the branding exercise.

Having a hypothesis exercise conducted is another important feature required when doing research. This hypothesis exercise will ensure the relevant information is market tested both from the credibility and results achieved by the use of the product.

The effort made to conduct the hypothesis exercise is to ensure without any room for doubt that the information used in the branding of the product is solidly grounded.

Gathering the relevant data to help understand the product and its hopeful impact on the consumer world is important to ensuring the success of its salability. Armed with this information the branding team will be able to focus on certain aspects of a product and use it to the optimum advantage to gain customer loyalty and satisfaction.

In conducting a complete research exercise the assigned team would also look into the competitors' success to understand the conditions tagged to its success. Only then will the research team be able to counter the competitors' success with their own styles.

Chapter 3:

Synopsis

Promoting services or products or one's self is pretty much the same thing. The only difference is in the style and type of promotion used. In order to be able to separate one's self from the rest and stand out favorably there are certain ideas or tip that can be followed.

It is not something to be taken lightly if individual want to get ahead in their careers or life in general. Relying on the merits of self promotion in order to distinguish one's self from the rest is sometimes the only thing that stands between failure and success.

Here are some of the tips to follow:

- The ability to identify and add value to portray one's self as an advantageous choice over others is important. This form of branding will ensure the potential client stays interested enough to enquire of the added value mentioned.

- Making a presentation form the added value angle with total confidence is another attractive feature to practice. The confidence shown will not only act as a plus point but will also impress the potential client. However coming on too strong could have the exact opposite negative results, as the confidence element maybe misconstrued as arrogance.

- Being able to "read" a situation or people and adjust the approach line accordingly is also advised. One sales pitch does not work for all circumstances. In being intuitive one is able to change game plans easily, quickly, and easily.

- Target the right people. Don't waste people's time with irrelevant information if the matter does not concern them. Doing this is unnecessary and also shows the ill informed state of the individual.

- Keep things short and simple, yet impactful. Being long winded with purposeful use of technically termed language can be very boring and annoying if it is not suitable conversation material for the listener.

Chapter 4:

Synopsis

Everyone and everything has some form of competitiveness tagged to it. In today's ever changing and fast moving world everyone is trying their best to get ahead using as many ways and means as possible. For some using the media is one option worth exploring.

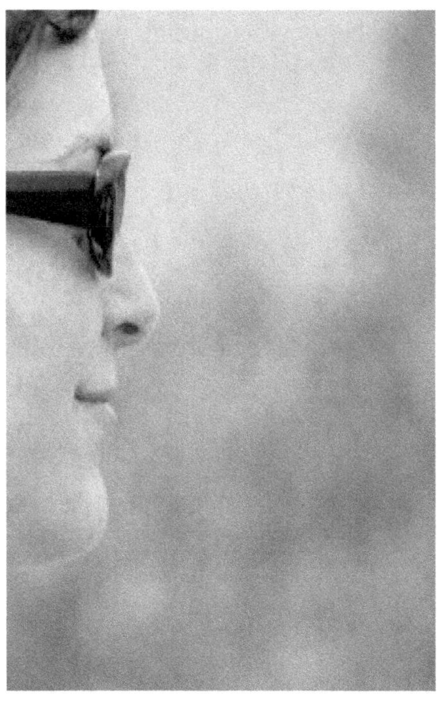

Get Your Name Out

In order to be recognized as an individual with outstanding or unusual or better that average qualities to present or promote, the first step to take is to reach the target audience quickly and effectively.

Finding the suitable "tools" to use for this self promotion to be a success is a necessary and important point to ponder upon. In identifying the right tools to use in order to reach the target audience, the path to success in being a recognizable entity is launched.

Most people tend to only bother or show some level of interest in the information or visual effects they are most exposed to. Therefore identifying the target audience one wishes to attract and then liking that information to the use of a suitable media tool will ensure the intended audience receives the self promoting information.

Smart media savvy individual will ensure they are constantly featured in the most popular media tools all the time. These tools may include the internet, blog sites, magazines, newspapers, flyers, and many others.

In creating the expose needed to stay relevant the individual is also engaging in the prospects in staying visible and encouraging others to be constantly reminded and aware of his or her existence. Going multimedia is one way of successfully reaching a wider audience platform. Using this form such as videos, audios and podcasts, images and others help to ensure the proper amount of exposure is garnered.

Creating the circumstances where questions and answers are entertained will also contribute to the relevance of the individual and also enhance exposure and popularity percentages.

Chapter 5:

Synopsis

Using the social media tool to network is a new and innovative means of communication. This form of communication allows individuals to connect, discover, and engage in various activities available through this channel. However there are certain dos and don'ts that needed to be adhered to in order for the successful interaction to prevail.

Today's Communication

When exploring the social media forms to make new contacts one must bear in mind that being short and precise is the key to holding the interest of the corresponding party.

Long winded and uninformative style of communications doesn't really encourage others to be interested to engage in building a connection.

Making the information posted as visual and as interesting as possible is a prerequisite in ensuring the interest levels of those targeted. Therefore having the mindset that less is more, is indeed wise when attempting to post information on the social media network.

Requiring a response of some sort is only natural but quite irrelevant and unnecessary. Though it may be thought of as rude or lacking in social etiquette generally people don't respond if there is no interest in establishing a communicative relationship.

Therefore one should be prepared for the possibility of not receiving any response at all to the efforts made in the exercise of trying to establish contact. Hence the advice, to state only relevant information and then to restrain from badgering the recipient for a response.

Making points as clear as possible in a concise form is also another prudent style of approach to use. Overwhelming the recipient with unnecessary information is annoying to say the least.

Also if there are any requests or requirements needed, it should be stated early on in the communication and not left to the end. Avoid giving the impression of being needy; instead try to be confident in the communication.

Chapter 6:

Synopsis

Using videos as an effective tool in branding, advertising, and self promotion is fast gaining popularity in the world of media today. Understanding the importance of the media contributions to the success of any endeavor is indeed practicing wisdom at its highest levels.

Visual Aids

Although using video facilities has been around for sometime it has yet to achieve the recognition it is merited. Those who use this form of media for networking, branding and advertising purposes understand its particular advantages.

Perhaps one very important reason to consider using video as a form of media exposure is the fact that most of the world's population today can relate to pictures and sounds.

Though reading the written word is still popular, a large percentage of media users prefer the visual form of acquiring the latest information as compared to having to spend time reading a fair bit of information to attain the same amount of information.

Besides being more pleasing to the eye, there are also a lot of other advantages that can be obtained by using video as a form of media communication.

The element of creativity can be explored without any inhibitions which may apply to the written word. By using video to get an idea or message across to the receiving party the creativity essence can be released, and this can take many forms like animations, projection filming, cartoon characters and many more.

All these contribute not only to the intensity of the intended message or idea, but also cater ideally to the interest of the current media savvy group of people.

- 21 -

From an eco friendly point of view, using video as a style of media presenting tools, the conservation of raw materials often used for advertising, branding, and self promotions can be decreased considerably. In adopting this method of media coverage the individual shows a lot of wisdom.

Chapter 7:

Synopsis

Sometimes in order to get the relevant information across to the public there is a need to take a further step in the media arena. This step taken is to provide the necessary training in any field connected to or in encouraging the use of the said product, service, or expertise in a particular field.

Offer Courses

When there is a launch of a new product that requires an in depth understanding of the uses and advantages of the product, the best way to encourage its use if through providing training courses. These training courses will allow the individual to learn about and be confident of the various uses of the product.

Training courses are also encouraged to help the individual be more confident in using, promoting, or simply taking about the product. It also encourages the individual to contribute by asking questions and satisfying all curiosity. Sometimes questions and scenarios can be put forth to further enhance the product and its chosen media coverage choice.

For the individual considering exploring this form of media communication, the use of the correct "tools" is also important. The level and consistency of the promotional material can be standardized, while its quality control can be monitored.

Training courses are currently offered for almost anything and is really quite accessible and affordable. When an individual has acquired these important bits of information through the training courses then they can impart this information to others.

Training courses are also a useful way of keeping abreast with the latest information and skills available. This will enable the individual to apply the newly learnt skills to the advantage and success of any chosen endeavor.

Through the success levels taught to achieve in the training courses, the course frame work also indirectly promotes the skills of the trainer for further branding and advertising purposes.

Chapter 8:

Provide Quality Material And Customer Service

Synopsis

As in any field, branding, advertising and media also follow similar guide lines to ensure its success levels. In order to have consistent success the issue of good quality material and customer service must be adequately addressed.

Do It Right

Good customer service in vital to creating a successful business environment. When potential customers are assured that they can and will get good service after the purchase of a product, the sale is much smoother and easier. Today customers want to be assured that there is still a relationship between the seller and buyer if and when there are issues that need to be addressed.

Making a sale is no longer the be all and end all of a customer and sales person contact. In promoting the customer service angle, a potential customer is shown the depth of the commitment practiced by the selling party.

Customers are more like to purchase product that have a good customer base service provider tool. More so today this particular feature is becoming almost a prerequisite for most customers.

Because of the vast variety of products available today, customers are becoming a more discerning bunch. Therefore the quality of the merchandise plays an important role as the deciding factor for the purchaser.

Taking the extra step to provide for all possible levels of quality ensure the success of the product sold. With the good quality elements tagged to the product or service, the chances of a new customer base is very good, as the old customers will indirectly promote the merits of the product. This type of promotion in invaluable to the success of any product and cannot be bought at any price.

Another advantage of providing quality material is that the integrity of the product and company promoting the product is maintained at its highest levels. Therefore any new ventures the said company decides to explore will be met will an eager and loyal customer base.

Chapter 9:

Synopsis

One way of ensuring the confidence and loyalty of potential customers is to utilize the product sold personally. When potential customers see the personal confidence placed on the product because of the personal use angle they will be more eager to try the product.

Get Involved

Also by using the product personally, one can confidently attest to its advantages and play down the disadvantages without seeming dishonest.

Personal experiences are always an invaluable element to inject into a sales pitch. In seeing the actual physical use and results of the product the potential customer is more likely to try the product with a more confident mind set, and therefore subconsciously adding to the success rate of the desired effects.

By encouraging all those involved in promoting the product to first be a user of the product the wisdom behind this thinking is that the style and demeanor applied during the sales pitch would be more convincing when compared to someone who does not use the product personally before attempting to sell it.

Also when the individual attempting to sell the product is already a user, it enables him or her to answer any questions about the product confidently and fairly accurately when questioned by a potential customer.

It is also a learning and discovering process for the user. Other advantages may be learnt and so contributing to the further enhancement towards the features of the said product.

From an advertising angle, using the product personally can also contribute to the making of a more realistic based advert.

The branding element will have added power behind the exercise if the fact is prominently advertised that the said product is used and happily accepted by its sellers. This kind of "free" advertising is similar to if not actually endorsing the capabilities of a product to its best advantage.

Chapter 10:

How Not Branding Can Spell Disaster

Synopsis

Because of the high costs incurred in the branding exercises a lot of companies shy away from using this method when reaching out to potential customers. The cost of a branding exercise also affects the final price of the said product.

What You Need To Know

Not branding a product is also not the best of ideas as there are a lot of relating factors that can cause the loss of potentially huge customer bases.

Branding contributes to the strength of the product in the market place where there is probably a variety of other products touting the same advantages in their products too. Therefore by using the branding method to capture the awareness of the potential customers, wisdom is shown, as it undoubtedly creates the brand presence in the target's mind.

To ensure the positive perception of the quality of the product, one needs that advantage to using branding. When the target customer base is focus on the advantages portrayed in the branding exercise, it is more than likely the potential customer will end up choosing the said product when the comparison is made to other limitedly or non existence of the branding element.

Disaster is very likely in terms of garnering the loyalty factor if branding is not used. With successful branding styles the seller is able to bank on the repeat behavior pattern of the customer base. This in turn will ensure long term success of the product with repeat usage and sales.

Wrapping Up

When branding is not used, and there are no loyalties fostered or involved, the emotional bonds that could possibly tie the customer to the product would be nonexistent.

Thus, causing a considerable amount of loss to the seller. Most successfully touted products use branding to suggest a certain image that would appeal to the potential customer.

The image portrayed by the branding exercise may encourage the customer to consider that particular product more favorably.